DISCLAIMER

The author disclaims any liability or responsibility for any consequences resulting from the use of the information in this book. The author generated some of the text in part with ChatGPT, OpenAI's large-scale language-generation model. Upon generating draft language, the author reviewed, edited, and revised the language to their own liking and takes ultimate responsibility for the content of this publication.

CHAPTER 1: INTRODUCTION

In the vast landscape of technological advancement, Artificial Intelligence (AI) stands as a transformative force with the potential to reshape societies, economies, and the very fabric of human existence. As we navigate the uncharted territories of the AI future, it becomes imperative to anchor our journey in ethical considerations and responsible development. This chapter sets the stage for understanding the multifaceted dimensions of the AI future, emphasizing the integration of AI technologies, the quest for efficiency, and the critical importance of ethical development.

1.1 The Rise of Artificial Intelligence

The journey of AI has been marked by unprecedented leaps in innovation, fueled by breakthroughs in machine learning, neural networks, and computational power. From self-learning algorithms to autonomous systems, AI has permeated various aspects of our daily lives, revolutionizing industries, healthcare, finance, and communication. As we stand on the cusp of a new era, characterized by the proliferation of AI applications, it is crucial to explore the opportunities and challenges that lie ahead.

1.2 Integration and Interconnectedness

The integration of AI into diverse domains is reshaping traditional paradigms and fostering a new era of interconnectedness. Smart cities, intelligent transportation systems, and automated supply chains exemplify the integration of AI into the very fabric of society. This interconnected landscape presents unparalleled opportunities for efficiency, innovation, and improved quality of life. However, it also raises ethical concerns related to privacy, security, and the potential for unintended consequences.

1.3 The Pursuit of Efficiency

One of the driving forces behind the widespread adoption of AI is the pursuit of efficiency. Automation, optimization, and data-driven decision-making have become key pillars in the quest for streamlined processes and enhanced productivity. While efficiency is a laudable goal, it demands careful consideration of the socio-economic implications, such as job displacement, economic inequality, and the ethical use of AI in decision-making processes that impact individuals and communities.

1.4 Ethical Considerations in AI Development

Ethics form the cornerstone of responsible AI development. As we empower machines with increasingly sophisticated capabilities, questions surrounding accountability, bias, transparency, and fairness become paramount. Chapter 1 delves into the ethical dimensions of AI, emphasizing the need for a collective commitment to principles that prioritize human well-being, societal harmony, and environmental sustainability.

1.5 Responsible AI Development: A Call to Action

The path forward in the AI future requires a proactive and principled approach. Responsible AI development entails collaboration among researchers, policymakers, industry leaders, and the broader society. This chapter concludes with a call to action, urging stakeholders to collectively shape the future of AI in a manner that aligns with ethical values, fosters inclusivity, and safeguards the well-being of present and future generations.

As we embark on this journey through the realms of AI, integration, efficiency, and ethical considerations will serve as guiding beacons, ensuring that our advancements contribute to a future that is not only technologically sophisticated but also ethically sound and sustainable.

CHAPTER 2: THE ETHICAL IMPERATIVE IN AI DEVELOPMENT

2.1 The Morality of Machines

The integration of AI into society raises profound questions about the moral implications of endowing machines with decision-making capabilities. As machines increasingly influence our daily lives, from autonomous vehicles making split-second decisions to algorithms shaping our online experiences, it becomes imperative to instill a sense of ethics into the heart of AI development. This chapter explores the ethical imperative of imbuing machines with a moral compass, examining the challenges and opportunities presented by aligning artificial intelligence with human values.

2.2 Accountability and Transparency

As AI systems become more sophisticated, understanding and assigning accountability becomes a complex challenge. Transparency in AI algorithms, decision-making processes, and data usage is paramount for fostering trust and accountability. This section delves into the importance of transparency as a cornerstone of ethical AI development, examining the need for clear communication about how AI systems operate and the implications of their actions.

2.3 Bias and Fairness in AI

The omnipresence of bias in AI algorithms has raised

concerns about discrimination and injustice. Whether it be in hiring processes, criminal justice systems, or healthcare, biased algorithms can perpetuate and exacerbate societal inequalities. This chapter explores the intricate relationship between bias, fairness, and AI, advocating for the development of algorithms that prioritize equitable outcomes and are sensitive to diverse perspectives.

2.4 Ethical Decision-Making in AI Systems

The ethical dimensions of AI extend beyond avoiding harm to actively promoting positive societal outcomes. This section investigates the concept of ethical decision-making in AI systems, emphasizing the importance of incorporating ethical frameworks into the very design and development of algorithms. It explores the role of interdisciplinary collaboration, bringing together ethicists, technologists, and domain experts to create AI systems that align with human values and societal well-being.

2.5 Privacy in the Age of AI

The increasing collection and analysis of vast amounts of personal data by AI systems pose significant challenges to individual privacy. This chapter examines the ethical considerations surrounding data privacy, emphasizing the need for robust safeguards, responsible data usage, and clear policies that protect individuals from unwarranted intrusions into their private lives.

2.6 Global Perspectives on AI Ethics

AI development is a global endeavor, and ethical considerations transcend geographical boundaries. This section explores diverse cultural, social, and legal perspectives on AI ethics, acknowledging the importance of a globally inclusive dialogue. It emphasizes the need for international collaboration in establishing ethical standards, frameworks, and guidelines that can guide the responsible development and deployment of AI technologies worldwide.

2.7 Toward Ethical AI Governance

To realize the ethical imperative in AI development, effective governance frameworks are essential. This chapter concludes with a discussion on the evolving landscape of AI governance, proposing strategies for the development of ethical guidelines, regulatory frameworks, and industry standards. It calls for a harmonized global effort to ensure that AI technologies serve humanity while respecting fundamental ethical principles.

As we navigate the complexities of AI ethics, Chapter 2 aims to shed light on the imperative of infusing morality into machines and building a future where artificial intelligence aligns seamlessly with human values, promoting a just, inclusive, and ethically conscious society.

CHAPTER 3: RESPONSIBLE AI INNOVATION AND DEVELOPMENT

3.1 Innovating with Purpose

In the rapidly evolving landscape of AI, innovation is a driving force that propels us into uncharted territories. However, innovation must be guided by a sense of purpose and responsibility. This chapter delves into the concept of responsible AI innovation, exploring how technological advancements can be harnessed to address societal challenges, enhance human well-being, and contribute to sustainable development.

3.2 Human-Centric Design Principles

The design of AI systems plays a pivotal role in shaping their impact on society. Human-centric design principles prioritize the needs, values, and experiences of individuals. This section examines the importance of designing AI systems with empathy, inclusivity, and user-centricity in mind. It explores methodologies that place humans at the center of the development process, ensuring that AI technologies enhance human capabilities without compromising ethical standards.

3.3 Ethical Considerations in AI Research

The foundations of responsible AI development are laid during the research phase. This chapter discusses the ethical considerations inherent in AI research, addressing issues such as data collection, experimental design, and the responsible handling of sensitive information. It emphasizes the importance of transparency in research practices and the need for ongoing ethical reviews to guide the trajectory of AI development.

3.4 Collaboration and Multidisciplinary Approaches

The complex nature of AI development requires collaboration across diverse fields. This section explores the benefits of multidisciplinary approaches, bringing together experts from fields such as ethics, sociology, psychology, and law to contribute their perspectives to AI development. By fostering collaboration, the aim is to create a holistic understanding of the societal impact of AI and develop solutions that are ethically sound and socially responsible.

3.5 Education and Ethical Literacy

Building a responsible AI future necessitates equipping developers, policymakers, and the broader public with ethical literacy. This chapter discusses the importance of education in AI ethics, advocating for the integration of ethical considerations into AI curricula. It explores how promoting ethical awareness and critical thinking can empower individuals to make informed decisions in the development and deployment of AI technologies.

3.6 Addressing Unintended Consequences

The development and deployment of AI can lead to unintended consequences, ranging from algorithmic biases to unforeseen societal shifts. This section addresses the challenge of anticipating and mitigating these unintended consequences. It explores strategies for ongoing monitoring, evaluation, and adaptation of AI systems to ensure they align with ethical principles and contribute positively to society.

3.7 Sustainable and Inclusive AI Development

Sustainability and inclusivity are integral components of responsible AI development. This chapter concludes by examining the importance of building AI systems that consider environmental impact, resource consumption, and inclusivity. It advocates for a future where AI technologies contribute to sustainable development goals, bridge societal divides, and empower diverse communities.

Chapter 3 envisions a future where innovation in AI is not only driven by technological prowess but is guided by a commitment to responsibility, inclusivity, and sustainability. By embracing these principles, we can navigate the complexities of AI development with a focus on creating positive, lasting impacts on society.

CHAPTER 4: LEGAL AND REGULATORY FRAMEWORKS FOR ETHICAL AI

4.1 The Need for Legal and Regulatory Oversight

As AI technologies continue to advance, the need for comprehensive legal and regulatory frameworks becomes increasingly apparent. This chapter delves into the evolving landscape of AI governance, examining the role of laws and regulations in ensuring ethical AI development, deployment, and use. It explores the challenges posed by the rapid pace of technological innovation and the imperative to establish legal structures that balance innovation with ethical considerations.

4.2 Defining Ethical Standards

The establishment of clear ethical standards is fundamental to the responsible development of AI. This section explores the process of defining and codifying ethical principles that guide AI research, development, and deployment. It discusses the role of industry standards, international collaborations, and governmental initiatives in setting ethical benchmarks to safeguard human rights, privacy, and societal values.

4.3 Accountability and Liability in AI

With the increasing autonomy of AI systems, questions of accountability and liability become complex. This chapter addresses the legal aspects of AI accountability, examining the challenges associated with attributing responsibility for AI actions. It explores potential legal frameworks that clarify liability issues, ensuring that developers, manufacturers, and users are held accountable for the ethical implications of AI technologies.

4.4 International Collaboration and Standards

AI development transcends national borders, requiring international collaboration to address ethical challenges effectively. This section discusses the importance of global cooperation in establishing common standards for AI ethics and regulation. It explores initiatives such as international treaties, collaborative research efforts, and cross-border regulatory frameworks aimed at fostering a harmonized approach to responsible AI development.

4.5 Privacy Laws and Data Protection

The vast amounts of data processed by AI systems raise significant privacy concerns. This chapter examines the role of privacy laws and data protection regulations in mitigating these concerns. It explores the challenges of balancing the need for data-driven innovation with the protection of individuals' privacy rights, highlighting the importance of robust legal frameworks to navigate this delicate balance.

4.6 Ethical Audits and Certification

To ensure compliance with ethical standards, there is a growing need for mechanisms such as ethical audits and certification processes. This section explores the concept of ethical audits, examining how organizations can undergo assessments to evaluate the ethical implications of their AI systems. It discusses the potential role of certification programs in providing transparency and assurance to users and stakeholders.

4.7 Adaptive Regulation for Emerging Technologies

The rapid evolution of AI requires regulatory frameworks that can adapt to emerging technologies and unforeseen challenges. This chapter concludes by examining the concept of adaptive regulation, exploring how legal frameworks can be designed to evolve alongside technological advancements. It emphasizes the importance of flexibility and responsiveness in regulatory approaches to effectively address the ethical considerations of AI in an ever-changing landscape.

In Chapter 4, we navigate the intricate intersections of law, ethics, and AI development, exploring the evolving legal and regulatory frameworks that play a crucial role in ensuring responsible and ethical AI practices. By establishing clear standards and fostering international collaboration, we aim to create a legal landscape that facilitates innovation while safeguarding ethical principles and societal well-being.

CHAPTER 5: BUILDING TRUST IN AI SYSTEMS

5.1 The Trust Deficit in AI

Trust is a cornerstone of successful AI integration into society. However, the opacity and complexity of AI algorithms often lead to a trust deficit among users and stakeholders. This chapter explores the importance of building and maintaining trust in AI systems, examining the factors that contribute to trust erosion and the strategies to foster transparency, accountability, and user confidence.

5.2 Transparency as a Trust-Building Measure

Transparency is a key element in building trust in AI systems. This section delves into the significance of transparent AI algorithms, decision-making processes, and data usage. It explores how open communication about the functioning of AI systems can demystify technology, empower users, and contribute to the establishment of trust in the broader community.

5.3 Explainability and Interpretability

The ability to explain AI decisions and actions is critical for trust-building. This chapter discusses the concepts of explainability and interpretability in AI, exploring methodologies that make AI systems more understandable to non-experts. It examines the challenges of balancing complexity with simplicity, ensuring that users can comprehend the reasoning behind AI-driven outcomes.

5.4 User Involvement and Feedback

Engaging users in the development process is essential for building trust. This section explores the importance of user involvement, feedback loops, and user-centric design in AI development. It advocates for inclusivity and collaboration with end-users to address concerns, preferences, and ensure that AI systems align with user expectations.

5.5 Ethical Communication and Marketing

How AI technologies are communicated and marketed significantly influences public perception. This chapter examines the role of ethical communication and marketing practices in building and maintaining trust. It explores strategies for transparently conveying the capabilities, limitations, and ethical considerations of AI systems to avoid hype, misinformation, or unrealistic expectations.

5.6 Robust Security and Privacy Measures

Security breaches and privacy concerns can erode trust in AI systems. This section explores the importance of robust cybersecurity measures and privacy protections. It discusses the role of encryption, secure data handling, and adherence to privacy regulations in building trust by ensuring the integrity and confidentiality of user data.

5.7 Continuous Monitoring and Accountability

Trust-building is an ongoing process that requires continuous monitoring and accountability. This chapter concludes by exploring the role of continuous assessment, auditing, and accountability mechanisms in maintaining trust in AI systems. It advocates for proactive measures to identify and rectify ethical issues, ensuring that AI technologies evolve responsibly and align with societal expectations.

Chapter 5 underscores the critical importance of trust in

the successful integration of AI into society. By focusing on transparency, explainability, user involvement, ethical communication, and robust security measures, we can foster a trusting relationship between users, developers, and AI systems, contributing to a future where AI is embraced with confidence and ethical considerations at the forefront.

CHAPTER 6: ETHICAL CONSIDERATIONS IN SPECIFIC AI APPLICATIONS

6.1 Healthcare: Balancing Innovation and Patient Well-being

The healthcare sector is witnessing a transformative impact from AI applications, ranging from diagnostics and personalized medicine to treatment recommendations. This chapter explores the ethical considerations inherent in AI-driven healthcare solutions, emphasizing the delicate balance between innovation, data privacy, and ensuring patient well-being. It examines issues related to bias in medical algorithms, informed consent, and the responsible use of sensitive health data.

6.2 Autonomous Vehicles: Navigating the Roads of Ethics

As autonomous vehicles become a reality, ethical considerations surrounding safety, decision-making, and accountability take center stage. This section delves into the ethical challenges posed by self-driving cars, addressing questions about algorithmic decision-making during critical situations, the prioritization of human safety, and the societal implications of widespread adoption. It explores the development of ethical frameworks for autonomous vehicle technologies to ensure responsible deployment.

6.3 Education: Augmenting Learning with Ethical AI

AI is increasingly integrated into educational systems, offering personalized learning experiences and innovative teaching tools. This chapter examines the ethical considerations in AI applications for education, exploring issues such as bias in educational algorithms, student privacy, and the potential impact on equality in access to educational resources. It emphasizes the need for ethical guidelines to harness AI's potential while safeguarding the principles of fairness and inclusivity in education.

6.4 Criminal Justice: Navigating Bias and Fairness

AI applications in criminal justice, including predictive policing and sentencing algorithms, raise significant ethical concerns related to bias and fairness. This section explores the challenges of ensuring fairness, transparency, and accountability in AI-driven criminal justice systems. It discusses the potential reinforcement of existing biases, the impact on marginalized communities, and the importance of ethical oversight to prevent unjust outcomes.

6.5 Finance: Striking the Balance between Innovation and Responsibility

In the financial industry, AI is revolutionizing processes such as risk assessment, fraud detection, and investment strategies. This chapter examines the ethical considerations in AI applications for finance, addressing issues of transparency, accountability, and the potential amplification of economic inequalities. It explores the development of ethical frameworks to guide the responsible use of AI in financial systems, ensuring stability and fairness.

6.6 Social Media: Ethical Challenges in Content Moderation

The pervasive influence of AI in social media platforms introduces ethical challenges in content moderation, user privacy, and the potential amplification of harmful content. This section explores the complex landscape of AI applications in social media, addressing issues such as algorithmic bias, the spread of misinformation, and the impact on user well-being. It advocates for ethical guidelines to mitigate the negative consequences and ensure responsible AI use in shaping online interactions.

6.7 Environmental Sustainability: AI's Role in a Greener Future

AI holds potential applications for addressing environmental challenges, from climate modeling to optimizing energy consumption. This chapter explores the ethical considerations in deploying AI for environmental sustainability, examining issues such as data privacy, the environmental impact of AI infrastructure, and the ethical use of AI to tackle global ecological challenges. It emphasizes the need for responsible AI development to contribute positively to environmental conservation.

Chapter 6 delves into the ethical considerations specific to various AI applications, recognizing the diverse impact AI has across different sectors. By addressing these considerations and developing sector-specific ethical guidelines, we can harness the benefits of AI technologies while mitigating potential risks and ensuring responsible and ethical deployment in various domains.

CHAPTER 7: THE ROLE OF STAKEHOLDERS IN ETHICAL AI DEVELOPMENT

7.1 The Diverse Landscape of Stakeholders

Ethical AI development involves a wide array of stakeholders, including researchers, developers, policymakers, industry leaders, users, and the broader public. This chapter explores the roles and responsibilities of different stakeholders in shaping the ethical trajectory of AI. It emphasizes the importance of collaboration and engagement to ensure a diverse range of perspectives and values are considered in the development and deployment of AI technologies.

7.2 Researchers and Developers: Ethical by Design

At the forefront of AI development, researchers and developers play a pivotal role in shaping the ethical landscape. This section delves into the ethical responsibilities of those involved in AI research and development, emphasizing the importance of ethical considerations at every stage. It explores the concept of "ethical by design," promoting the integration of ethical principles into the very fabric of AI technologies from their inception.

7.3 Policymakers: Shaping the Regulatory Landscape

Policymakers play a crucial role in creating the legal and regulatory frameworks that guide AI development and deployment. This chapter examines the responsibilities of policymakers in addressing ethical considerations, fostering innovation, and safeguarding public interests. It discusses the challenges of keeping regulations agile in the face of rapid technological advancements and the importance of international collaboration in establishing ethical standards.

7.4 Industry Leaders: Driving Ethical Innovation

Industry leaders wield significant influence in shaping the ethical landscape of AI. This section explores the responsibilities of corporations and tech giants in driving ethical innovation. It discusses the role of corporate policies, ethical guidelines, and responsible business practices in ensuring that AI technologies align with societal values, contribute to positive outcomes, and avoid negative impacts on users and communities.

7.5 Users: Empowering Ethical Adoption

Users are integral stakeholders in the ethical deployment of AI technologies. This chapter examines the role of users in shaping AI outcomes, advocating for informed decision-making, and holding developers and organizations accountable. It explores the importance of user awareness, education, and feedback in fostering a culture of responsible AI use.

7.6 Civil Society and Advocacy Groups: Ensuring Accountability

Civil society and advocacy groups play a crucial role in holding stakeholders accountable for ethical AI practices. This section explores how these entities contribute to public awareness, scrutinize AI systems for potential biases or ethical lapses, and advocate for transparency and accountability. It emphasizes the importance of a vigilant civil society in ensuring that AI technologies serve the greater good.

7.7 Global Collaboration: Navigating Ethical Consensus

Given the global nature of AI development, international collaboration is essential in navigating ethical consensus. This chapter concludes by examining the role of global cooperation in establishing common ethical standards and frameworks. It emphasizes the need for open dialogue, shared principles, and collaborative efforts to address cross-border ethical considerations and ensure responsible AI development on a global scale.

Chapter 7 underscores the interconnectedness of stakeholders in the ethical development of AI. By acknowledging and fulfilling their respective responsibilities, stakeholders can collectively contribute to a future where AI technologies align with ethical principles, benefit society, and minimize potential harms.

CHAPTER 8: ETHICAL CHALLENGES AND OPPORTUNITIES IN EMERGING AI TECHNOLOGIES

8.1 Quantum Computing: The Ethical Frontier

As quantum computing emerges as a transformative technology, it brings forth a new set of ethical challenges and opportunities. This chapter explores the ethical considerations surrounding quantum computing, including issues of data security, algorithmic transparency, and the potential societal impacts of unprecedented computational power. It examines how ethical frameworks can guide the responsible development and deployment of quantum computing technologies.

8.2 Brain-Computer Interfaces: Navigating the Mind Ethically

Advancements in brain-computer interfaces (BCIs) raise profound ethical questions about privacy, consent, and cognitive autonomy. This section delves into the ethical challenges and opportunities presented by BCIs, exploring issues such as mental privacy, potential misuse, and the impact on individual identity. It emphasizes the importance of ethical guidelines to ensure the responsible development and ethical use of these emerging technologies.

8.3 AI in Human Augmentation: Enhancing Ethical Considerations

The integration of AI in human augmentation technologies, from prosthetics to cognitive enhancements, introduces ethical complexities. This chapter examines the ethical considerations surrounding AI-driven human augmentation, addressing issues of consent, equality, and the potential societal divide between enhanced and non-enhanced individuals. It explores the need for ethical frameworks to guide the responsible integration of AI in human augmentation technologies.

8.4 Swarm Intelligence and Autonomous Systems: Coordinating Ethically

Swarm intelligence and autonomous systems, inspired by collective behavior in nature, present ethical challenges related to coordination, decision-making, and societal impact. This section explores the ethical considerations in deploying autonomous swarms, drones, and robotic systems. It discusses issues of accountability, transparency, and the potential consequences of widespread adoption. Ethical guidelines are proposed to ensure responsible development and deployment of these emerging technologies.

8.5 AI in Space Exploration: Ethical Frontiers Beyond Earth

The use of AI in space exploration introduces unique ethical challenges and opportunities. This chapter examines the ethical considerations related to AI-driven space missions, autonomy in extraterrestrial environments, and the potential impact on space ecosystems. It explores the need for ethical frameworks to guide the responsible use of AI in space exploration, ensuring sustainability and respect for cosmic environments.

8.6 AI in Creativity: Navigating Artistic and Ethical Boundaries

As AI becomes a tool for creative endeavors, including art, music, and literature, it raises questions about authorship, creativity, and ethical boundaries. This section explores the ethical considerations in AI-generated content, addressing issues such as intellectual property, cultural appropriation, and the role of human creators. It advocates for ethical guidelines to navigate the intersection of AI and creativity responsibly.

8.7 Ethical Considerations in AI for Global Challenges

AI is increasingly leveraged to address global challenges such as climate change, healthcare disparities, and humanitarian crises. This chapter concludes by examining the ethical considerations in using AI for global challenges. It explores issues related to accessibility, inclusivity, and the responsible use of AI in addressing pressing global issues. Ethical frameworks are proposed to guide the development and deployment of AI solutions that contribute positively to humanity's collective well-being.

Chapter 8 explores the ethical challenges and opportunities in emerging AI technologies, recognizing the dynamic landscape of technological innovation. By proactively addressing these ethical considerations, we can ensure that the development and deployment of emerging AI technologies contribute positively to society while minimizing potential risks and harms.

CHAPTER 9: ETHICAL CONSIDERATIONS IN AI GOVERNANCE AND POLICY

9.1 The Imperative for Ethical AI Governance

As AI continues to evolve, the need for robust governance and policy frameworks becomes increasingly critical. This chapter explores the ethical considerations in AI governance and policy, emphasizing the role of regulatory bodies, international collaboration, and the development of guidelines to ensure responsible and ethical AI development, deployment, and use.

9.2 Regulatory Challenges in a Rapidly Changing Landscape

The fast-paced evolution of AI technology poses challenges for regulatory bodies striving to keep pace with innovation. This section delves into the regulatory challenges associated with AI, including the need for agility, adaptability, and the ability to address emerging ethical concerns. It discusses strategies for creating regulatory frameworks that balance innovation with ethical considerations and outlines the challenges of enforcement in a global context.

9.3 International Collaboration for Ethical AI

Given the global nature of AI development, international

collaboration is essential for establishing common ethical standards. This chapter examines the importance of collaborative efforts among nations, international organizations, and industry stakeholders to create a unified approach to AI governance. It explores the challenges and opportunities of building a consensus on ethical guidelines that transcend geographical boundaries.

9.4 Balancing Innovation and Ethical Oversight

The delicate balance between fostering innovation and ensuring ethical oversight is a central theme in AI governance. This section explores strategies for achieving this balance, discussing the role of regulatory sandboxes, adaptive frameworks, and ongoing dialogue between regulators and industry stakeholders. It emphasizes the importance of creating an environment that encourages innovation while safeguarding against potential ethical pitfalls.

9.5 Public-Private Partnerships in AI Governance

Public-private partnerships are instrumental in addressing the multifaceted challenges of AI governance. This chapter explores the collaborative efforts between governments, industry leaders, and non-governmental organizations to establish ethical standards and guidelines. It discusses the role of these partnerships in fostering transparency, accountability, and responsible AI practices.

9.6 Ethical Considerations in AI Policy Development

The formulation of AI policies requires a deep understanding of ethical considerations. This section examines the ethical dimensions of policy development, addressing issues such as inclusivity, fairness, and the protection of fundamental rights. It explores strategies for incorporating diverse perspectives into policy-making processes and ensuring that policies align with ethical principles and societal values.

9.7 Building Ethical AI Governance Capacities

Effective AI governance requires the development of capacities within regulatory bodies and institutions. This chapter concludes by exploring the need for building ethical AI governance capacities, including training programs, interdisciplinary collaboration, and the integration of ethical expertise into regulatory frameworks. It emphasizes the importance of creating a skilled and informed governance ecosystem to navigate the ethical challenges of AI responsibly.

Chapter 9 underscores the critical role of ethical considerations in AI governance and policy. By addressing the challenges associated with regulatory frameworks, fostering international collaboration, and building capacities for ethical governance, we can create an environment that promotes responsible AI development and ensures that technological advancements align with ethical principles and societal values.

CHAPTER 10: THE FUTURE OF ETHICAL AI: CHALLENGES AND ASPIRATIONS

10.1 The Evolving Ethical Landscape

As AI technologies continue to advance, the ethical landscape is dynamic and evolving. This chapter explores the future of ethical AI, considering the challenges and aspirations that lie ahead. It examines how ongoing technological developments, societal shifts, and ethical considerations will shape the trajectory of AI in the years to come.

10.2 Anticipating Ethical Challenges in AI Evolution

The rapid evolution of AI introduces new challenges and complexities. This section anticipates future ethical challenges in AI, including issues related to advanced AI capabilities, the integration of AI in novel domains, and the potential for unforeseen consequences. It discusses the importance of proactive ethical anticipation and strategies for mitigating risks in the ever-changing AI landscape.

10.3 Societal Impacts and Ethical Considerations

AI's impact on society is multifaceted, influencing aspects of work, privacy, and human relationships. This chapter explores the societal impacts of AI and the associated ethical considerations. It considers questions of economic equity, cultural shifts, and the need for inclusive policies that address the potential societal disparities arising from AI advancements.

10.4 Aspirations for Ethical AI: Inclusivity and Accessibility

The future of ethical AI envisions a landscape that is inclusive and accessible to diverse populations. This section discusses aspirations for AI that prioritize inclusivity, ensuring that the benefits of technology are equitably distributed across different demographics. It explores strategies for reducing biases, promoting diversity in AI development, and addressing the digital divide to create a more inclusive technological future.

10.5 Striving for Ethical AI Education and Literacy

Education and literacy in AI ethics are crucial for navigating the ethical challenges of the future. This chapter examines the aspirations for enhancing ethical AI education, ensuring that individuals across various disciplines are equipped with the knowledge and skills to make informed decisions. It discusses the role of educational institutions, industry, and governments in fostering a culture of ethical awareness and responsibility.

10.6 Ethical AI and Environmental Sustainability

Environmental sustainability is an increasingly prominent consideration in AI development. This section explores aspirations for ethical AI that align with environmental conservation goals. It discusses strategies for minimizing the carbon footprint of AI technologies, optimizing energy usage, and promoting sustainable practices to ensure that AI contributes positively to the global effort to address climate change.

10.7 Ethical AI Governance in a Global Context

The global nature of AI development necessitates aspirations for effective and harmonized ethical AI governance. This chapter concludes by discussing the aspirations for global cooperation, collaborative governance structures, and shared ethical standards. It explores the potential for international alliances to address ethical challenges on a global scale, ensuring that AI technologies are developed and deployed responsibly across borders.

Chapter 10 reflects on the evolving ethical landscape of AI, considering the challenges and aspirations that will shape its future trajectory. By anticipating ethical challenges, prioritizing inclusivity, promoting ethical education, addressing environmental sustainability, and fostering global cooperation in AI governance, we can aspire to create a future where AI technologies contribute positively to humanity while upholding ethical principles.

CHAPTER 11: BEYOND ETHICS: AI AND HUMAN VALUES

11.1 The Human-Centric Approach

As AI technologies become increasingly integrated into our lives, a human-centric approach becomes paramount. This chapter explores the importance of aligning AI with fundamental human values, emphasizing the need to prioritize human well-being, dignity, and autonomy. It delves into the ethical dimensions of AI development that go beyond mere compliance, aiming to create technologies that enhance human values and contribute positively to society.

11.2 Dignity and Autonomy in AI

Respecting human dignity and autonomy is a foundational ethical principle in AI development. This section examines the challenges and aspirations related to upholding human dignity and autonomy in the age of AI. It explores issues of consent, individual agency, and the potential impacts of AI on personal freedoms. Aspirations include the development of AI systems that empower individuals, respect their autonomy, and preserve their dignity.

11.3 Societal Harmony and Inclusivity

AI's impact on societal harmony and inclusivity is a crucial consideration. This chapter explores aspirations for AI technologies that foster social cohesion, bridge divides, and promote inclusivity. It discusses strategies for addressing biases, promoting diversity in AI development teams, and creating technologies that contribute to a more harmonious and inclusive society.

11.4 Trust as a Foundation

Trust is the bedrock of any successful relationship between humans and AI systems. This section delves into the aspirations for establishing and maintaining trust in AI technologies. It explores strategies for transparent communication, explainability, and user involvement to build and sustain trust. Aspirations include a future where users can trust AI systems to act ethically, predictably, and in their best interests.

11.5 Fairness and Equity in AI

The pursuit of fairness and equity is central to ethical AI development. This chapter examines aspirations for AI systems that actively contribute to reducing societal disparities and biases. It discusses the importance of fairness in algorithmic decision-making, addressing historical inequities, and fostering a future where AI promotes social justice and equal opportunities for all.

11.6 Empowerment through Ethical AI

AI has the potential to empower individuals and communities. This section explores aspirations for AI technologies that empower users by providing them with meaningful insights, enhancing their capabilities, and supporting informed decision-making. It discusses the ethical dimensions of empowerment and the responsibility of AI developers to create technologies that amplify human potential while mitigating risks.

11.7 A Holistic Perspective: Ethical AI in Everyday Life

The final chapter concludes by presenting a holistic perspective on ethical AI in everyday life. It underscores the interconnected aspirations of aligning AI with human values, promoting dignity and autonomy, fostering societal harmony, building trust, ensuring fairness, and empowering individuals. By adopting a comprehensive ethical framework, we aspire to create a future where AI technologies enrich human experiences while upholding the core values that define us as individuals and as a society.

CHAPTER 12: ETHICAL AI IN PRACTICE: CASE STUDIES AND LESSONS LEARNED

12.1 Case Studies in Ethical AI Implementation

This chapter explores real-world case studies of ethical AI implementation across various industries and applications. It examines instances where organizations have successfully navigated ethical challenges and incorporated responsible AI practices into their operations. The case studies provide insights into the practical application of ethical principles, shedding light on both successful approaches and lessons learned.

12.2 Healthcare: Ethical AI in Diagnostics and Treatment

In the healthcare sector, the implementation of AI in diagnostics and treatment presents unique ethical considerations. This section delves into case studies that highlight ethical challenges and successful strategies in healthcare AI. It explores issues such as patient consent, data privacy, and the responsible deployment of AI technologies to improve medical outcomes while maintaining ethical standards.

12.3 Finance: Navigating Ethical Considerations in Algorithmic Trading

Algorithmic trading in the financial industry involves complex ethical considerations. This part of the chapter explores case studies in finance, examining the challenges of algorithmic decision-making, market manipulation risks, and the impact on economic fairness. It discusses ethical solutions and lessons learned from implementing responsible AI practices in the financial sector.

12.4 Education: Ethical Implementation of AI in Learning Environments

The use of AI in educational settings presents ethical challenges related to student privacy, algorithmic biases, and the digital divide. This section explores case studies that showcase ethical AI implementation in education, highlighting successful approaches to personalized learning, inclusive practices, and the responsible use of student data.

12.5 Criminal Justice: Balancing Equity and Accountability

The implementation of AI in criminal justice systems raises ethical concerns about bias, transparency, and fairness. This part of the chapter examines case studies in criminal justice, illustrating ethical challenges and successful initiatives. It explores efforts to address bias in predictive policing algorithms, ensure transparency in decision-making, and uphold accountability in AI-driven criminal justice applications.

12.6 Social Media: Addressing Misinformation and Algorithmic Bias

Social media platforms face ethical challenges related to the spread of misinformation, algorithmic biases, and their impact on user well-being. This section explores case studies that delve into ethical considerations in social media AI implementation. It examines efforts to combat misinformation, enhance content moderation practices, and promote user safety in the digital realm.

12.7 Lessons Learned and Best Practices

The final part of the chapter synthesizes the lessons learned from the case studies and identifies best practices for ethical AI implementation. It explores common themes, successful strategies, and key takeaways across diverse industries. By analyzing real-world examples, this chapter aims to provide valuable insights for organizations and practitioners seeking to implement ethical AI in their respective domains.

Chapter 12 reflects on the practical implementation of ethical AI principles through case studies, offering valuable lessons and best practices. By learning from real-world experiences, organizations can gain insights into effective strategies for navigating ethical challenges and fostering responsible AI development and deployment.

CHAPTER 13: THE CONTINUOUS EVOLUTION OF ETHICAL AI

13.1 The Dynamic Nature of Ethical Challenges

As AI technologies evolve, so do the ethical challenges associated with their development and deployment. This chapter explores the dynamic nature of ethical considerations in AI, acknowledging that new challenges will inevitably emerge as technology advances. It discusses the importance of continuous vigilance, adaptability, and proactive ethical frameworks to address evolving ethical concerns.

13.2 Anticipating Future Ethical Dilemmas

In the ever-changing landscape of AI, anticipating and preparing for future ethical dilemmas is crucial. This section delves into the process of scenario planning and ethical foresight, aiming to identify potential ethical challenges before they arise. It discusses methodologies for anticipating future dilemmas, fostering a proactive approach to ethics in AI development, and staying ahead of emerging ethical concerns.

13.3 Ethical Considerations in Emerging Technologies

As new technologies emerge, they bring forth novel ethical

considerations. This part of the chapter explores the ethical dimensions of cutting-edge technologies, including but not limited to advanced AI, quantum computing, and neurotechnologies. It discusses strategies for addressing ethical challenges in emerging technologies, ensuring that ethical principles are integrated into the fabric of innovation.

13.4 The Role of Ethical Audits and Impact Assessments

To maintain ethical standards in AI development, the use of ethical audits and impact assessments becomes imperative. This section examines the role of ethical audits and impact assessments in continuously evaluating the ethical implications of AI technologies. It explores how these mechanisms can be employed to identify and address ethical challenges throughout the lifecycle of AI systems.

13.5 Feedback Loops and Continuous Improvement

Continuous improvement is a cornerstone of ethical AI development. This chapter discusses the importance of feedback loops in gathering insights from users, stakeholders, and the broader public. It explores how continuous feedback can inform the refinement of AI systems, ensuring that they evolve responsibly and remain aligned with ethical principles over time.

13.6 Incorporating Ethical Considerations in Design Iterations

Ethical considerations should be an integral part of the design and development process of AI systems. This section emphasizes the importance of incorporating ethical principles in design iterations, fostering a culture where ethical discussions are ongoing and integrated into decision-making processes. It explores strategies for ensuring that ethical considerations are not an afterthought but a core element of the design phase.

13.7 Collaborative Ethical Governance for Future AI

The future of ethical AI requires collaborative governance that involves stakeholders from diverse backgrounds. This part of the chapter explores the concept of collaborative ethical governance, advocating for inclusive decision-making processes that consider the perspectives of researchers, developers, policymakers, users, and ethicists. It discusses the importance of fostering a shared sense of responsibility and accountability in shaping the ethical trajectory of AI.

Chapter 13 envisions a future where ethical AI is a continuous, adaptive process that responds to the evolving challenges presented by advancing technologies. By embracing ethical foresight, incorporating feedback loops, and fostering collaborative governance, the aim is to create a future where AI technologies evolve responsibly and ethically, contributing positively to society.

CHAPTER 14: GLOBAL PERSPECTIVES ON ETHICAL AI

14.1 The Globalization of AI Ethics

As AI technologies transcend borders, the ethical considerations associated with their development and deployment become global in nature. This chapter explores the globalization of AI ethics, acknowledging the diverse perspectives, cultural nuances, and regulatory approaches that shape ethical considerations across different regions. It discusses the challenges and opportunities of fostering a globally informed approach to ethical AI.

14.2 Cultural Variations in Ethical Frameworks

Different cultures have distinct ethical frameworks and values that influence perspectives on AI ethics. This section delves into the cultural variations in ethical considerations, examining how societal norms, traditions, and philosophical perspectives shape the ethical discourse around AI. It discusses the importance of cultural sensitivity in developing global ethical standards and fostering cross-cultural understanding in AI development.

14.3 Legal and Regulatory Diversity

The legal and regulatory landscape for AI varies significantly from one jurisdiction to another. This part of the chapter explores the diversity in AI-related laws and regulations globally, addressing issues such as data protection, privacy, and accountability. It discusses the challenges posed by this diversity and the potential benefits of harmonizing international efforts to create a cohesive ethical framework.

14.4 International Collaboration in Ethical AI

The global nature of AI necessitates international collaboration to address ethical challenges effectively. This section examines initiatives, collaborations, and partnerships among nations, international organizations, and industry stakeholders to promote ethical AI practices on a global scale. It explores the potential for shared ethical standards, collaborative research, and the exchange of best practices to shape the ethical trajectory of AI worldwide.

14.5 Ethical Considerations in AI Diplomacy

AI diplomacy is an emerging field that addresses the international dimensions of AI ethics. This chapter discusses the role of diplomatic efforts in shaping ethical considerations, fostering collaboration, and mitigating ethical challenges associated with AI on the global stage. It explores the potential for diplomatic initiatives to promote ethical norms and guidelines for responsible AI development.

14.6 Human Rights and Ethical AI

The intersection of AI and human rights is a critical aspect of global AI ethics. This section examines how AI technologies can impact human rights and explores the ethical considerations related to privacy, freedom of expression, and non-discrimination. It discusses the importance of upholding human rights in the development and deployment of AI globally.

14.7 Ethical AI and Sustainable Development Goals

Aligning AI development with the United Nations Sustainable Development Goals (SDGs) is an aspirational approach to global

AI ethics. This part of the chapter explores how AI can contribute positively to achieving the SDGs and addresses the ethical considerations associated with AI applications in areas such as healthcare, education, environmental sustainability, and poverty alleviation. It discusses the potential for AI to be a force for good on a global scale.

Chapter 14 provides insights into the global perspectives on ethical AI, acknowledging the diversity of ethical frameworks, legal landscapes, and cultural considerations across different regions. By fostering international collaboration, respecting human rights, and aligning AI with global sustainability goals, the aim is to create a shared ethical framework that promotes responsible AI development and deployment worldwide.

CHAPTER 15: ETHICAL AI: PUBLIC PERCEPTION AND ENGAGEMENT

15.1 The Role of Public Perception

Public perception plays a crucial role in shaping the ethical discourse around AI. This chapter explores the dynamics of public perception and its impact on the ethical considerations of AI development and deployment. It examines the factors that influence how the public views AI technologies, the role of media, and the implications for ethical practices in the AI industry.

15.2 Public Awareness and Education

Promoting public awareness and education about AI is essential for fostering an informed and engaged society. This section delves into the importance of educating the public about AI technologies, their capabilities, and potential ethical implications. It explores strategies for transparent communication, public outreach, and educational initiatives to empower individuals to make informed decisions about AI.

15.3 Ethical Considerations in Media Representation

Media plays a significant role in shaping public perceptions of AI. This part of the chapter examines the ethical considerations in media representation of AI technologies, exploring how portrayals in the media can influence public understanding, fears, and expectations. It discusses the responsibility of media outlets in providing accurate, balanced, and ethical coverage of AI developments.

15.4 Public Engagement in AI Decision-Making

Engaging the public in AI decision-making processes is a key aspect of ethical governance. This section explores the importance of public participation, consultation, and input in shaping AI policies, regulations, and deployment strategies. It discusses the challenges and benefits of involving diverse perspectives from the public in decision-making forums related to AI ethics.

15.5 Ethical Considerations in AI Product Design

The design of AI products can influence how users perceive and interact with technology. This chapter examines the ethical considerations in AI product design, including issues of transparency, user consent, and the prevention of bias. It discusses the responsibility of AI developers and designers to prioritize ethical considerations in the design phase to build trust and meet user expectations.

15.6 Addressing Ethical Concerns and Fears

Public perception of AI is often influenced by concerns and fears about job displacement, loss of privacy, and the potential misuse of technology. This section explores strategies for addressing and mitigating these ethical concerns. It discusses the importance of proactively addressing public fears, fostering understanding, and implementing safeguards to build trust in AI technologies.

15.7 Participatory Ethical Governance: A Vision for the Future

The chapter concludes by envisioning a future where participatory ethical governance involves the public in shaping the trajectory of AI development. It explores the potential for inclusive, transparent, and collaborative approaches that incorporate public values and preferences into the ethical governance of AI. This vision aims to create a society where AI technologies align with human values and priorities.

Chapter 15 sheds light on the crucial role of public perception and engagement in the ethical considerations of AI. By promoting public awareness, fostering education, addressing concerns, and involving the public in decision-making processes, the aim is to build a foundation for ethical AI development that reflects societal values and priorities.

CHAPTER 16: ETHICAL AI IN THE FUTURE WORKPLACE

16.1 The Transformative Impact of AI on the Workplace

As AI technologies continue to evolve, their impact on the future workplace is transformative. This chapter explores the ethical considerations surrounding the integration of AI in the workplace, addressing issues related to job displacement, worker well-being, and the responsible use of AI to enhance productivity and innovation.

16.2 Job Displacement and Reskilling Initiatives

The introduction of AI technologies may lead to job displacement in certain sectors. This section examines the ethical considerations surrounding job displacement and explores strategies for reskilling and upskilling initiatives to equip workers with the necessary skills for the evolving job market. It discusses the responsibility of employers and policymakers to mitigate the impact of AI on employment.

16.3 Worker Well-being and Mental Health

The integration of AI in the workplace raises ethical concerns related to worker well-being and mental health. This part of the chapter explores the potential stressors and challenges associated with AI technologies in the workplace. It discusses the importance of fostering a healthy work environment, promoting work-life balance, and addressing ethical considerations to ensure the well-being of employees.

16.4 Ethical Use of AI for Performance Evaluation

AI is increasingly used for performance evaluation and decision-making in the workplace. This section delves into the ethical considerations surrounding the use of AI algorithms for employee assessments, promotions, and compensation. It explores issues related to transparency, fairness, and the prevention of algorithmic bias in performance evaluations.

16.5 Ensuring Fairness and Diversity in Hiring Practices

AI is often utilized in hiring processes, raising ethical considerations related to fairness and diversity. This chapter examines the ethical challenges associated with AI-driven recruitment tools and explores strategies for ensuring fairness, preventing bias, and promoting diversity in hiring practices. It discusses the responsibility of organizations to implement ethical hiring solutions.

16.6 Ethical Considerations in AI-mediated Collaboration

As AI facilitates collaboration in the workplace, ethical considerations emerge in areas such as communication, decision-making, and team dynamics. This section explores the challenges and opportunities of AI-mediated collaboration, emphasizing the importance of transparent communication, inclusive decision-making, and ethical practices to enhance teamwork and productivity.

16.7 Ethical Frameworks for Future Workplace AI

The chapter concludes by discussing the need for ethical frameworks that guide the integration of AI in the future workplace. It explores the development of guidelines, policies, and best practices to ensure responsible AI use, protect worker rights, and foster a workplace environment that upholds ethical principles. This vision for ethical AI in the future workplace aims to balance technological advancements with ethical considerations, creating a positive and inclusive work environment.

CHAPTER 17: ETHICAL AI IN EDUCATION: NURTURING RESPONSIBLE DIGITAL LEARNING ENVIRONMENTS

17.1 The Integration of AI in Education

AI technologies are increasingly being integrated into educational environments, offering new opportunities and challenges. This chapter explores the ethical considerations surrounding the use of AI in education, addressing issues related to student privacy, bias in algorithms, and the responsible implementation of AI to enhance learning experiences.

17.2 Student Privacy and Data Protection

The use of AI in education often involves the collection and analysis of student data, raising ethical concerns about privacy and data protection. This section examines the importance of safeguarding student privacy, obtaining informed consent, and implementing secure data practices. It discusses the ethical responsibilities of educational institutions and technology providers in protecting the sensitive information of students.

17.3 Bias and Fairness in Educational Algorithms

AI algorithms in educational settings can inadvertently perpetuate bias and inequality. This part of the chapter explores the ethical considerations related to bias in educational algorithms, emphasizing the need for fairness, transparency, and accountability. It discusses strategies for identifying and mitigating bias to ensure that AI technologies contribute to equitable learning opportunities for all students.

17.4 Responsible Use of AI for Personalized Learning

AI enables personalized learning experiences, tailoring educational content to individual student needs. This section delves into the ethical considerations of personalized learning, exploring issues such as algorithmic decision-making, student autonomy, and the potential impact on educational outcomes. It discusses the responsible use of AI to enhance personalized learning while respecting ethical principles.

17.5 Ensuring Inclusivity and Accessibility

AI in education should strive for inclusivity and accessibility to ensure that all students, regardless of background or ability, can benefit from technological advancements. This chapter examines the ethical considerations related to inclusivity and accessibility, discussing strategies for designing AI-powered educational tools that cater to diverse learning needs and promote equal opportunities for students.

17.6 Ethical Considerations in EdTech Research

Research in educational technology (EdTech) involving AI raises ethical considerations regarding informed consent, data transparency, and the potential impact on students. This section explores the ethical dimensions of EdTech research, emphasizing the importance of ethical review processes, transparency in research methodologies, and the responsible dissemination of research findings in the academic community.

17.7 Fostering Digital Literacy and Ethical Education

Promoting digital literacy and ethical education is essential to prepare students for responsible engagement with AI technologies. The chapter concludes by discussing the ethical imperative of integrating digital literacy and ethical education into curricula. It explores strategies for empowering students to understand the ethical implications of AI, make informed decisions, and navigate the digital landscape responsibly.

Chapter 17 envisions a future where AI in education is implemented ethically, fostering responsible digital learning environments that prioritize student privacy, equity, and inclusivity. By addressing the ethical considerations associated with AI in education, this chapter aims to guide educators, policymakers, and technology developers in creating positive and equitable learning experiences for students.

CHAPTER 18: ETHICAL AI IN HEALTHCARE: BALANCING INNOVATION AND PATIENT WELL-BEING

18.1 The Transformative Role of AI in Healthcare

AI technologies have the potential to revolutionize healthcare, offering new possibilities for diagnostics, treatment, and patient care. This chapter explores the ethical considerations surrounding the integration of AI in healthcare, addressing issues related to patient privacy, medical decision-making, and the responsible use of AI to improve health outcomes.

18.2 Patient Privacy and Data Security

The use of AI in healthcare involves the processing of sensitive patient data, raising ethical concerns about privacy and data security. This section examines the importance of safeguarding patient privacy, ensuring informed consent, and implementing robust data security measures. It discusses the ethical responsibilities of healthcare providers and technology developers in protecting patient information.

18.3 Ethical Considerations in AI-assisted Diagnosis and Treatment

AI-assisted diagnosis and treatment tools have the potential to enhance medical decision-making, but they also raise ethical considerations. This part of the chapter explores the ethical dimensions of AI in healthcare, addressing issues such as transparency in algorithms, patient autonomy, and the responsible integration of AI into clinical practices. It discusses strategies for ensuring ethical use of AI in diagnosis and treatment.

18.4 Bias and Fairness in Healthcare Algorithms

Bias in healthcare algorithms can lead to disparities in patient outcomes and treatment plans. This section examines the ethical considerations related to bias and fairness in healthcare algorithms, emphasizing the need for equity, transparency, and accountability. It discusses strategies for identifying and mitigating bias to ensure that AI technologies contribute to fair and inclusive healthcare practices.

18.5 Informed Consent and Shared Decision-making

Informed consent and shared decision-making are critical components of ethical healthcare practices. This chapter delves into the ethical considerations surrounding the use of AI in supporting informed consent and facilitating shared decision-making between healthcare providers and patients. It discusses the importance of transparency, patient education, and involving patients in the decision-making process.

18.6 Addressing Ethical Challenges in Telemedicine

Telemedicine, enabled by AI technologies, presents unique ethical challenges related to remote patient care and digital health services. This section explores the ethical considerations in telemedicine, including issues of accessibility, quality of care, and the responsible deployment of AI in virtual healthcare settings. It discusses strategies for addressing ethical challenges to ensure equitable and effective telemedicine practices.

18.7 Ensuring Equity in AI-driven Healthcare Innovations

The chapter concludes by discussing the ethical imperative of ensuring equity in AI-driven healthcare innovations. It explores strategies for addressing healthcare disparities, promoting accessibility, and fostering inclusivity in the development and deployment of AI technologies in healthcare. The goal is to create a future where AI contributes positively to healthcare outcomes while upholding ethical principles and patient well-being.

CHAPTER 19: ETHICAL IMPLICATIONS OF AI IN LAW ENFORCEMENT AND CRIMINAL JUSTICE

19.1 The Intersection of AI and Law Enforcement

The integration of AI technologies in law enforcement and criminal justice systems raises complex ethical considerations. This chapter explores the ethical implications of AI in policing, surveillance, and legal decision-making, addressing issues related to privacy, bias, accountability, and the responsible use of AI to ensure justice and public safety.

19.2 Privacy Concerns in AI-powered Surveillance

AI-powered surveillance tools have the potential to impact individual privacy and civil liberties. This section examines the ethical considerations surrounding the use of AI in surveillance, discussing issues such as facial recognition technology, mass data collection, and the implications for personal privacy rights. It explores strategies for balancing the need for public safety with ethical considerations in surveillance practices.

19.3 Bias and Fairness in Predictive Policing Algorithms

Predictive policing algorithms, powered by AI, have been criticized for perpetuating bias and discrimination. This part of the chapter delves into the ethical considerations related to bias and fairness in predictive policing, exploring the challenges of algorithmic decision-making in law enforcement. It discusses strategies for identifying and mitigating bias to ensure fair and equitable outcomes.

19.4 Accountability and Transparency in AI-driven Legal Decision-making

AI technologies are increasingly involved in legal decision-making processes, raising questions about accountability and transparency. This section explores the ethical considerations in using AI for legal decisions, such as sentencing and risk assessments. It discusses the importance of transparency, explainability, and accountability to ensure that AI-driven legal processes align with ethical principles and the rule of law.

19.5 Ethical Challenges in Autonomous Weapons and Robotic Policing

The deployment of autonomous weapons and robotic policing technologies introduces ethical challenges in terms of accountability, human rights, and the potential for misuse. This chapter examines the ethical considerations in AI-driven weapons and robotic policing, discussing issues related to lethal autonomous systems and the responsible use of technology in law enforcement.

19.6 Community Engagement and Ethical Policing

Ethical policing involves engaging with communities to build trust, address concerns, and ensure accountability. This section explores the importance of community engagement in the context of AI in law enforcement. It discusses strategies for fostering transparent communication, involving the public in decision-making processes, and addressing community concerns to build ethical policing practices.

19.7 The Role of Ethics in Criminal Justice Reform

The chapter concludes by discussing the role of ethics in driving criminal justice reform efforts. It explores how ethical considerations can contribute to the development of fair and just criminal justice systems, emphasizing the importance of transparency, accountability, and the responsible use of AI to address systemic issues and promote ethical practices in law enforcement and criminal justice.

CHAPTER 20: ETHICAL CONSIDERATIONS IN AI FOR ENVIRONMENTAL SUSTAINABILITY

20.1 The Role of AI in Environmental Sustainability

AI technologies have the potential to play a significant role in addressing environmental challenges and promoting sustainability. This chapter explores the ethical considerations associated with the use of AI for environmental sustainability, examining issues related to resource management, climate change mitigation, and the responsible deployment of AI to support ecological conservation efforts.

20.2 Data Privacy and Environmental Monitoring

AI applications for environmental monitoring often involve the collection and analysis of vast amounts of data, raising ethical concerns about privacy and data security. This section examines the importance of ensuring data privacy in environmental monitoring efforts, addressing issues related to informed consent, data transparency, and the responsible handling of sensitive environmental data.

20.3 Ethical Considerations in AI for Climate Change Modeling

AI is increasingly used in climate change modeling to analyze complex environmental data and predict future trends. This part of the chapter explores the ethical considerations surrounding AI applications in climate change research, including issues related to accuracy, transparency, and the responsible communication of scientific findings. It discusses strategies for ensuring ethical practices in AI-driven climate modeling.

20.4 Balancing Technological Advancements with Environmental Impact

While AI has the potential to contribute to environmental sustainability, its own environmental impact must be considered. This section examines the ethical considerations related to the carbon footprint of AI technologies, exploring strategies for minimizing energy consumption, optimizing algorithms, and promoting sustainable practices in AI development and deployment.

20.5 Responsible AI in Natural Resource Management

AI applications in natural resource management, such as precision agriculture and water conservation, raise ethical considerations about equitable access, environmental justice, and the responsible use of technology. This chapter explores the ethical dimensions of AI in natural resource management, discussing issues related to inclusivity, fairness, and the potential social and environmental impacts of AI-driven resource management.

20.6 Ethical Challenges in Wildlife Conservation and Biodiversity Monitoring

The use of AI in wildlife conservation and biodiversity monitoring introduces ethical challenges related to privacy, animal welfare, and the potential disruption of ecosystems. This section delves into the ethical considerations surrounding AI applications in conservation efforts, exploring strategies for balancing conservation goals with ethical practices and the well-being of wildlife.

20.7 Fostering Ethical Practices in AI-driven Environmental Initiatives

The chapter concludes by discussing the importance of fostering ethical practices in AI-driven environmental initiatives. It explores the role of transparency, collaboration, and community engagement in ensuring that AI technologies contribute positively to environmental sustainability. By addressing ethical considerations in the development and deployment of AI for environmental purposes, the aim is to create a future where technology supports ecological conservation and promotes a sustainable relationship with the natural world.

CHAPTER 21: THE ETHICAL LANDSCAPE OF AI IN FINANCE

21.1 The Impact of AI on the Financial Industry

The integration of AI in the financial industry has transformative implications, from algorithmic trading to personalized financial services. This chapter explores the ethical considerations surrounding the use of AI in finance, addressing issues related to transparency, accountability, and the responsible deployment of AI to enhance financial services while safeguarding ethical principles.

21.2 Transparency and Explainability in Algorithmic Trading

Algorithmic trading, powered by AI, raises ethical concerns related to transparency and explainability. This section examines the importance of transparency in financial algorithms, addressing issues such as market manipulation, insider trading risks, and the responsible use of AI in algorithmic trading to ensure fairness and market integrity.

21.3 Fair Lending Practices and AI-powered Credit Scoring

AI is increasingly used in credit scoring and lending decisions, introducing ethical considerations related to fairness and inclusivity. This part of the chapter explores the ethical dimensions of AI-powered credit scoring, discussing issues such as algorithmic bias, discrimination, and the responsible use of technology to ensure fair lending practices and financial inclusion.

21.4 Privacy and Security in AI-driven Financial Services

The use of AI in financial services involves the processing of sensitive financial data, raising ethical concerns about privacy and security. This section examines the ethical considerations related to data protection, customer privacy, and the responsible handling of financial information in AI-driven financial services. It discusses strategies for safeguarding customer data and ensuring secure financial transactions.

21.5 Ethical Challenges in Robo-Advisors and Automated Financial Planning

Robo-advisors and automated financial planning tools powered by AI present ethical challenges related to trust, accountability, and the potential impact on investor outcomes. This chapter explores the ethical considerations in the use of AI for financial advice, addressing issues such as algorithmic decision-making, fiduciary responsibility, and the responsible deployment of technology to enhance financial planning services.

21.6 Regulatory Compliance and Ethical Standards in Fintech

The fast-paced evolution of fintech introduces challenges in regulatory compliance and adherence to ethical standards. This section examines the ethical considerations in the fintech industry, exploring issues related to regulatory frameworks, consumer protection, and the responsible development and deployment of AI technologies in financial innovation.

21.7 The Role of Ethical Leadership in Financial Organizations

The chapter concludes by discussing the role of ethical leadership in financial organizations. It explores how leaders can foster a culture of ethical decision-making, transparency, and responsible innovation in the integration of AI in finance. By prioritizing ethical considerations, financial leaders can contribute to the development of a sustainable and ethical future for the financial industry.

64

CHAPTER 22: THE ETHICAL DIMENSIONS OF AI IN SOCIAL MEDIA

22.1 The Impact of AI on Social Media

AI technologies play a significant role in shaping the landscape of social media, influencing content distribution, user interactions, and information dissemination. This chapter explores the ethical considerations associated with the use of AI in social media, addressing issues related to privacy, misinformation, algorithmic biases, and the responsible deployment of AI to enhance user experiences while safeguarding ethical principles.

22.2 User Privacy and Data Security in Social Media

Social media platforms rely on user data to personalize content and enhance user experiences, raising ethical concerns about privacy and data security. This section examines the ethical considerations related to user privacy, informed consent, and data security in the context of AI-driven social media platforms. It discusses strategies for protecting user privacy and ensuring secure data practices.

22.3 Ethical Challenges in Content Moderation

AI is increasingly used in content moderation on social media platforms, introducing ethical challenges related to censorship, freedom of expression, and the prevention of online harm. This part of the chapter explores the ethical dimensions of content moderation, discussing issues such as algorithmic biases, transparency, and the responsible use of AI to address harmful content while respecting user rights.

22.4 Addressing Misinformation and Algorithmic Bias

The spread of misinformation on social media and algorithmic biases in content recommendations pose ethical challenges that require attention. This section examines the ethical considerations related to misinformation and bias in AI algorithms, discussing strategies for identifying and mitigating false information, promoting media literacy, and ensuring fairness in content distribution.

22.5 User Empowerment and Control in AI-driven Social Media

AI-driven social media platforms have the potential to empower users with personalized experiences, but this empowerment should come with user control and transparency. This chapter explores the ethical considerations related to user empowerment and control, addressing issues such as algorithmic transparency, user preferences, and the responsible design of AI features that prioritize user agency.

22.6 Inclusivity and Diversity in Social Media Algorithms

Algorithmic biases in social media algorithms can impact inclusivity and diversity, perpetuating existing societal biases. This section examines the ethical considerations related to inclusivity and diversity in AI-driven social media, discussing strategies for promoting diverse perspectives, addressing biases, and fostering inclusive digital spaces for users from all backgrounds.

22.7 Responsible Innovation and Ethical Design in Social Media AI

The chapter concludes by discussing the importance of responsible innovation and ethical design in social media AI. It explores how social media platforms can prioritize ethical considerations in the development and deployment of AI technologies, emphasizing transparency, user engagement, and the responsible use of AI to create a positive and ethical social media environment.

CHAPTER 23: ETHICAL AI IN GOVERNANCE: ENSURING ACCOUNTABILITY AND TRANSPARENCY

23.1 The Role of AI in Governance

The integration of AI technologies in governance introduces new opportunities and challenges. This chapter explores the ethical considerations associated with the use of AI in government processes, addressing issues related to accountability, transparency, fairness, and the responsible deployment of AI to enhance public services while safeguarding ethical principles.

23.2 Accountability in Automated Decision-making

Automated decision-making processes powered by AI in government operations raise ethical concerns about accountability and responsibility. This section examines the ethical considerations related to accountability in AI-driven governance, discussing issues such as algorithmic decision-making, public oversight, and the responsible use of technology to ensure fair and just outcomes.

23.3 Transparency and Explainability in Government AI Systems

The transparency and explainability of AI systems in government are crucial for fostering trust and accountability. This part of the chapter explores the ethical dimensions of transparency and explainability in government AI systems, addressing issues related to open governance, accessibility of information, and the responsible communication of AI-driven decisions to the public.

23.4 Ethical Considerations in AI-assisted Policy Formulation

AI technologies are increasingly utilized in policy formulation, introducing ethical considerations related to fairness, inclusivity, and the potential impact on diverse communities. This section examines the ethical dimensions of AI-assisted policy development, discussing issues such as stakeholder engagement, bias mitigation, and the responsible use of technology to create inclusive and equitable policies.

23.5 Bias and Fairness in Government AI Applications

The potential for bias in government AI applications, from law enforcement to social services, requires careful consideration of fairness and equity. This chapter explores the ethical considerations related to bias and fairness in government AI applications, discussing strategies for identifying and mitigating biases to ensure that AI technologies contribute to equitable public services.

23.6 Citizen Engagement and Inclusive Decision-making

Incorporating citizen engagement and inclusive decision-making processes are essential aspects of ethical governance. This section examines the ethical considerations related to citizen engagement in the context of AI-driven governance, discussing issues such as participatory decision-making, transparency, and the responsible use of AI to facilitate inclusive and democratic processes.

23.7 Ensuring Ethical AI Procurement and Deployment

The chapter concludes by discussing the importance of

ensuring ethical AI procurement and deployment in government operations. It explores how governments can adopt ethical guidelines, prioritize responsible AI vendors, and foster a culture of ethical decision-making to ensure that AI technologies align with public values and contribute positively to governance.

CHAPTER 24: THE FUTURE OF AI ETHICS: EMERGING TRENDS AND FRONTIERS

24.1 The Evolving Landscape of AI Ethics

The field of AI ethics is dynamic, with emerging trends and frontiers shaping the future of responsible AI development and deployment. This chapter explores the evolving landscape of AI ethics, highlighting emerging trends, challenges, and opportunities that will influence the ethical considerations of AI in the years to come.

24.2 Ethical Considerations in Advanced AI Systems

As AI systems advance, from sophisticated machine learning models to autonomous systems, new ethical considerations arise. This section examines the ethical challenges associated with advanced AI systems, discussing issues related to autonomy, decision-making, and the responsible integration of advanced AI technologies into various domains.

24.3 Human Augmentation and Ethical Boundaries

The concept of human augmentation, where AI technologies enhance human capabilities, introduces ethical questions about boundaries, consent, and the potential societal impact. This part of the chapter explores the ethical considerations in human augmentation, discussing issues related to privacy, identity, and the responsible use of AI to augment human abilities.

24.4 Ethical Dimensions of Neurotechnologies

Advancements in neurotechnologies, including brain-computer interfaces and neural implants, raise ethical considerations about privacy, cognitive enhancement, and the potential for unintended consequences. This section examines the ethical dimensions of neurotechnologies, discussing issues related to informed consent, neuroprivacy, and the responsible development and deployment of AI-driven innovations in neuroscience.

24.5 The Intersection of AI and Creativity

The integration of AI in creative fields, from art to music composition, introduces ethical considerations related to originality, authorship, and the collaborative nature of AI-human creative processes. This chapter explores the ethical dimensions of AI in creativity, discussing issues such as intellectual property, cultural impact, and the responsible use of AI as a tool for artistic expression.

24.6 Ethical Considerations in Human-AI Relationships

As humans interact with AI systems more intimately, the ethical dimensions of human-AI relationships become increasingly significant. This section examines the ethical considerations in human-AI relationships, discussing issues related to trust, empathy, and the responsible design of AI systems that prioritize positive and meaningful interactions with humans.

24.7 Global Collaboration in AI Ethics Research

The chapter concludes by discussing the importance of global collaboration in AI ethics research. It explores the need for interdisciplinary research, international partnerships, and shared efforts to address ethical challenges on a global scale. By fostering collaboration, the aim is to create a future where ethical principles guide the development and deployment of AI technologies, ensuring a positive and inclusive impact on society.

CHAPTER 25: ETHICAL LEADERSHIP IN THE AI ERA

25.1 The Role of Ethical Leadership

In the era of AI, ethical leadership becomes crucial in guiding organizations, policymakers, and technology developers toward responsible and ethical AI development and deployment. This chapter explores the role of ethical leadership in shaping the trajectory of AI technologies, addressing the principles, practices, and responsibilities that ethical leaders must uphold.

25.2 Setting Ethical Standards and Frameworks

Ethical leaders play a key role in setting and promoting ethical standards and frameworks for AI development and deployment. This section examines the responsibilities of ethical leaders in establishing clear ethical guidelines, principles, and frameworks that guide organizations and industries in the responsible use of AI technologies.

25.3 Fostering a Culture of Ethical Decision-Making

Creating a culture of ethical decision-making is essential in organizations working with AI. This part of the chapter explores how ethical leaders can foster a culture where ethical considerations are integral to decision-making processes. It discusses the importance of communication, education, and accountability in cultivating an ethical organizational culture.

25.4 Addressing Bias and Diversity in AI Teams

Ethical leaders must address issues of bias and lack of diversity in AI development teams to ensure that diverse perspectives are considered in the creation of AI technologies. This section examines the responsibilities of ethical leaders in promoting diversity, equity, and inclusion in AI teams, and addressing biases to create more ethical and robust AI systems.

25.5 Advocating for Transparency and Accountability

Transparency and accountability are core principles in ethical AI development. Ethical leaders advocate for transparency in AI systems, ensuring that decisions made by algorithms are explainable and understandable. This part of the chapter discusses how ethical leaders can champion accountability in AI systems, both within their organizations and in the broader industry.

25.6 Balancing Innovation with Ethical Considerations

Ethical leaders face the challenge of balancing innovation and ethical considerations in the development of AI technologies. This section explores how ethical leaders can foster innovation while ensuring that ethical principles are prioritized. It discusses the importance of ethical risk assessments and the responsible deployment of AI innovations.

25.7 Collaborative Approaches to Ethical Leadership

The chapter concludes by emphasizing the collaborative nature of ethical leadership in the AI era. Ethical leaders must collaborate with other organizations, policymakers, researchers, and the broader community to address the complex ethical challenges posed by AI technologies. By working together, ethical leaders can contribute to the creation of a more responsible and ethical AI landscape.

CHAPTER 26: NAVIGATING ETHICAL CHALLENGES IN AI RESEARCH

26.1 The Ethical Landscape of AI Research

AI research plays a fundamental role in shaping the capabilities and impact of AI technologies. This chapter explores the ethical challenges inherent in AI research, examining issues related to transparency, reproducibility, dual-use concerns, and the responsible conduct of research to ensure positive outcomes for society.

26.2 Transparency and Open Science in AI Research

Transparency and open science are critical principles in AI research to ensure the reproducibility of results and foster trust within the scientific community. This section examines the ethical considerations related to transparency in AI research, discussing the importance of sharing methodologies, data, and code to promote open and collaborative scientific practices.

26.3 Dual-Use Dilemmas in AI Research

The dual-use nature of AI technologies raises ethical dilemmas regarding the potential for both beneficial and harmful applications. This part of the chapter explores the ethical considerations related to dual-use concerns in AI research, discussing how researchers can navigate the challenges of anticipating and mitigating potential negative impacts of their work.

26.4 Ethical Responsibilities in Publication and Communication

Researchers have ethical responsibilities in the publication and communication of their findings to ensure the responsible dissemination of knowledge. This section examines the ethical dimensions of publishing AI research, addressing issues such as clear communication, avoiding sensationalism, and considering the potential societal impacts of research outcomes.

26.5 Addressing Bias and Fairness in AI Research

AI research must grapple with the ethical challenges associated with bias and fairness in algorithms and models. This chapter discusses the responsibilities of researchers in addressing bias, promoting fairness, and conducting thorough evaluations to ensure that AI technologies are equitable and do not perpetuate or exacerbate existing societal biases.

26.6 Ethical Review Processes in AI Research

Ethical review processes are crucial to assess the potential ethical implications of AI research. This section explores the role of ethical review boards and committees in evaluating research proposals, ensuring the protection of human subjects, and addressing ethical considerations associated with the development and experimentation of AI technologies.

26.7 Collaborative and Interdisciplinary Approaches

Collaborative and interdisciplinary approaches are essential to navigating the ethical challenges in AI research. The chapter concludes by emphasizing the importance of collaboration among researchers, ethicists, policymakers, and other stakeholders. By fostering interdisciplinary dialogue and collaboration, the AI research community can work collectively to address ethical concerns and promote the responsible advancement of AI technologies.

CHAPTER 27: ETHICAL CONSIDERATIONS IN AI REGULATION AND POLICY

27.1 The Imperative for AI Regulation

As AI technologies continue to advance, the need for robust regulation and policy frameworks becomes imperative to ensure responsible development and deployment. This chapter explores the ethical considerations in AI regulation and policymaking, addressing issues related to accountability, transparency, and the establishment of guidelines to govern AI technologies.

27.2 Establishing Ethical Guidelines for AI Development

Ethical guidelines are crucial in providing a framework for the responsible development of AI technologies. This section examines the importance of establishing ethical guidelines for AI development, discussing the principles that should guide regulatory efforts to ensure that AI technologies align with ethical standards and societal values.

27.3 Accountability Mechanisms in AI Regulation

Ensuring accountability is a key aspect of effective AI regulation. This part of the chapter explores the ethical considerations related to accountability mechanisms, discussing the roles of regulatory bodies, compliance frameworks, and the establishment of clear lines of responsibility in governing the development and deployment of AI technologies.

27.4 Transparency Requirements for AI Systems

Transparency is fundamental to building trust in AI systems and informing the public about how AI technologies are used. This section examines the ethical considerations related to transparency requirements in AI regulation, discussing the need for clear communication, disclosure, and transparency in the design and operation of AI systems.

27.5 Ethical Use of AI in Critical Applications

AI applications in critical areas such as healthcare, criminal justice, and finance require special attention in regulation due to their significant societal impact. This chapter discusses the ethical considerations in regulating the use of AI in critical applications, emphasizing the importance of responsible AI deployment and adherence to ethical standards.

27.6 Ensuring Fairness and Non-Discrimination

AI regulation must address the ethical imperative of ensuring fairness and preventing discrimination in the use of AI technologies. This section explores the considerations related to fairness and non-discrimination in AI regulation, discussing strategies for identifying and mitigating biases to create more equitable AI systems.

27.7 International Collaboration in AI Governance

The chapter concludes by emphasizing the importance of international collaboration in AI governance. Ethical considerations in AI regulation are not confined to national borders, and global collaboration is crucial in addressing the complex challenges posed by AI technologies. By working together, countries and international organizations can create a cohesive and ethical framework for the responsible development and use of AI technologies on a global scale.

CHAPTER 28: THE ETHICAL FUTURE: SHAPING A POSITIVE PATH FORWARD

28.1 The Evolution of AI Ethics

The journey of AI ethics has witnessed significant developments, challenges, and advancements. This chapter reflects on the evolution of AI ethics, acknowledging the progress made and the ongoing efforts to address ethical considerations in AI development and deployment. It sets the stage for envisioning a positive and ethical future for AI technologies.

28.2 Learning from Ethical Challenges

The ethical challenges encountered in the development and deployment of AI technologies offer valuable lessons. This section explores the insights gained from past challenges, emphasizing the importance of continuous learning, adaptation, and the iterative refinement of ethical frameworks to address emerging issues and promote responsible AI practices.

28.3 Toward Inclusive and Accessible AI

The ethical future of AI envisions inclusivity and accessibility, ensuring that the benefits of AI technologies are accessible to diverse populations. This part of the chapter explores strategies for fostering inclusivity, addressing digital divides, and promoting equitable access to AI advancements to prevent the exacerbation of existing societal inequalities.

28.4 Ethical Innovation and Human-Centric Design

Ethical innovation and human-centric design principles are crucial for shaping the future of AI in a positive direction. This section discusses the importance of prioritizing ethical considerations in the innovation process, embracing human-centric design principles, and placing human well-being at the forefront of AI development.

28.5 Strengthening Global Collaboration

Global collaboration is essential in addressing the ethical challenges of AI on an international scale. This chapter explores the potential for strengthened collaboration among countries, organizations, researchers, and policymakers to develop common ethical standards, share best practices, and collectively navigate the complex landscape of AI ethics.

28.6 Empowering Ethical Leadership

Ethical leadership plays a pivotal role in steering the future of AI technologies. This section discusses the qualities and responsibilities of ethical leaders in the AI era, emphasizing their role in fostering a culture of ethical decision-making, transparency, and accountability across organizations and industries.

28.7 Engaging Society in Ethical Discourse

Engaging society in ethical discourse is vital for creating an inclusive and informed approach to AI development and deployment. The chapter concludes by exploring the importance of involving the public in ethical discussions, incorporating diverse perspectives, and ensuring that societal values contribute to shaping the ethical future of AI technologies.

CHAPTER 29: THE ROLE OF EDUCATION IN AI ETHICS

29.1 The Crucial Role of Education

Education plays a pivotal role in shaping the ethical landscape of AI. This chapter explores how educational institutions, from schools to universities and beyond, can contribute to fostering ethical awareness, responsible practices, and a deeper understanding of AI ethics among students, professionals, and the broader public.

29.2 Integrating AI Ethics into Curricula

To prepare future generations for ethical engagement with AI, educational curricula must incorporate AI ethics as a core component. This section examines the importance of integrating AI ethics into curricula across disciplines, fostering a multidisciplinary approach that equips learners with the knowledge and skills to navigate the ethical dimensions of AI technologies.

29.3 Developing Ethical Awareness and Critical Thinking

Education in AI ethics goes beyond imparting knowledge; it involves cultivating ethical awareness and critical thinking skills. This part of the chapter explores strategies for developing these essential attributes among students, enabling them to critically assess the ethical implications of AI technologies and make informed decisions.

29.4 Promoting Diversity and Inclusivity in AI Education

To ensure a holistic understanding of AI ethics, education must promote diversity and inclusivity. This section discusses the importance of incorporating diverse perspectives, voices, and experiences in AI education, creating an inclusive learning environment that reflects the societal impact and ethical considerations associated with AI technologies.

29.5 Encouraging Ethical Research and Innovation

Educational institutions play a key role in fostering ethical research and innovation in the field of AI. This chapter explores how educators can encourage students to conduct research and pursue innovation with a strong ethical foundation, promoting responsible practices that prioritize societal well-being and ethical considerations.

29.6 Ethical Leadership Development

Educational programs have the opportunity to nurture future leaders with a strong ethical foundation. This section discusses the role of education in developing ethical leaders in the AI sector, emphasizing the importance of instilling ethical values, promoting responsible decision-making, and preparing students to lead with integrity in the evolving landscape of AI.

29.7 Lifelong Learning and Adaptability

Given the dynamic nature of AI technologies, fostering a culture of lifelong learning and adaptability is crucial. The chapter concludes by exploring how education can instill a commitment to continuous learning and adaptability among individuals in the AI workforce. Lifelong learning ensures that professionals stay informed about evolving ethical standards and contribute to the responsible development of AI throughout their careers.

CHAPTER 30: BEYOND ETHICS: AI AND SOCIETAL IMPACT

30.1 The Broader Impact of AI on Society

AI technologies extend beyond ethical considerations to have profound societal impacts. This chapter explores the multifaceted ways in which AI shapes and influences society, addressing economic, cultural, and political dimensions. It delves into the challenges and opportunities presented by AI in various societal realms.

30.2 Economic Implications of AI

The integration of AI into the workforce has significant economic implications. This section examines the effects of AI on employment, job markets, and economic structures. It explores strategies for addressing challenges such as job displacement, income inequality, and the need for reskilling in the face of AI-driven economic transformations.

30.3 Cultural and Social Transformations

AI influences cultural and social dynamics by shaping communication, entertainment, and societal norms. This part of the chapter explores how AI impacts cultural production, social interactions, and the dissemination of information. It discusses the challenges and opportunities associated with AI-driven cultural and social transformations.

30.4 Political and Governance Challenges

The deployment of AI technologies introduces challenges in the political and governance spheres. This section examines how AI influences political processes, decision-making, and governance structures. It discusses the ethical considerations and potential risks associated with the intersection of AI and political systems, emphasizing the need for responsible governance in the AI era.

30.5 Privacy in the Age of AI

AI's extensive use in data processing raises significant privacy concerns. This chapter explores the implications of AI on personal privacy, surveillance practices, and the ethical considerations surrounding the collection and use of personal data. It discusses strategies for safeguarding privacy rights in the age of AI.

30.6 Addressing Bias and Discrimination

Beyond ethical considerations, AI has the potential to exacerbate societal biases and discrimination. This section examines the challenges of bias and discrimination in AI systems, discussing strategies for identifying, mitigating, and preventing biases to ensure that AI technologies contribute to a fair and equitable society.

30.7 The Future of Human-AI Collaboration

The chapter concludes by exploring the future of human-AI collaboration. It discusses the potential for AI to enhance human capabilities, foster collaboration, and contribute positively to societal development. The aim is to envision a future where AI technologies are harnessed for the betterment of society, guided by ethical principles and a commitment to addressing the broader societal impacts of AI.

CHAPTER 31: ANTICIPATING AI'S FUTURE: RISKS AND MITIGATIONS

31.1 The Uncertain Path of AI Development

As AI continues to advance, uncertainties and risks emerge that necessitate careful consideration. This chapter explores potential future risks associated with AI development and deployment, providing insights into the challenges that may arise and proposing strategies for mitigating these risks to ensure a positive and responsible trajectory for AI technologies.

31.2 Unintended Consequences of AI

The rapid evolution of AI technologies may lead to unintended consequences. This section examines the potential risks and negative outcomes that could arise from AI development, discussing the importance of foresight, impact assessments, and proactive measures to anticipate and address unintended consequences.

31.3 Ethical and Security Concerns in AI

As AI becomes more integrated into critical systems, ethical and security concerns become paramount. This part of the chapter explores the potential ethical and security challenges associated with the widespread adoption of AI, discussing strategies for addressing these concerns and ensuring that AI technologies are deployed responsibly.

31.4 The Impact of AI on Employment

AI's impact on the job market raises concerns about unemployment and job displacement. This section examines the potential risks associated with AI-related changes in employment and explores strategies for mitigating these risks, including reskilling initiatives, workforce adaptation, and the development of supportive policies.

31.5 AI and Autonomous Systems: Safety Challenges

The deployment of autonomous systems powered by AI introduces safety challenges. This chapter discusses the risks associated with AI-driven autonomous systems, including self-driving vehicles and drones, and explores strategies for ensuring the safety and reliability of these systems through rigorous testing, regulations, and responsible development practices.

31.6 Global Governance for AI

The lack of a comprehensive global governance framework for AI poses risks in terms of coordination, standards, and ethical guidelines. This section explores the challenges associated with global governance of AI and discusses potential approaches to fostering international collaboration, setting standards, and developing ethical principles on a global scale.

31.7 The Importance of Ethical Leadership

Ethical leadership plays a crucial role in mitigating the risks associated with AI development. The chapter concludes by emphasizing the importance of ethical leadership in navigating the uncertainties of AI's future. Ethical leaders can guide organizations, policymakers, and researchers in addressing challenges, promoting responsible practices, and ensuring that AI technologies contribute positively to society.

CHAPTER 32: SHAPING AI GOVERNANCE: POLICIES FOR A RESPONSIBLE FUTURE

32.1 The Imperative for Effective AI Governance

The dynamic and transformative nature of AI technologies necessitates the development of robust governance policies. This chapter explores the imperative for effective AI governance, addressing the challenges and opportunities in crafting policies that ensure responsible AI development, deployment, and impact on society.

32.2 Crafting Comprehensive AI Governance Frameworks

Comprehensive AI governance frameworks are essential for providing clear guidelines on the ethical, legal, and societal dimensions of AI technologies. This section examines the components of effective AI governance frameworks, including principles, regulations, and standards that organizations and policymakers can adopt to promote responsible AI practices.

32.3 Regulatory Approaches to AI: Striking the Right Balance

Regulating AI involves finding the right balance between fostering innovation and addressing ethical concerns. This part of the chapter explores various regulatory approaches to AI, discussing how policymakers can strike a balance that encourages technological advancement while safeguarding against potential risks and harms associated with AI deployment.

32.4 International Cooperation in AI Governance

Given the global nature of AI technologies, international cooperation is crucial in establishing consistent and effective governance mechanisms. This section discusses the importance of collaboration among nations, organizations, and stakeholders to develop harmonized AI governance standards, share best practices, and address transnational challenges associated with AI.

32.5 Ethical Considerations in AI Policy Development

AI policies must be grounded in ethical considerations to ensure responsible development and deployment. This chapter examines the ethical dimensions of AI policy development, discussing the principles and values that should underpin policies to address societal concerns, protect individual rights, and foster a positive impact on communities.

32.6 Adaptable Policies for Evolving AI Technologies

The rapid evolution of AI technologies requires policies that are adaptable and responsive to change. This section explores strategies for developing agile and flexible AI policies that can effectively address emerging challenges, technological advancements, and shifts in societal expectations over time.

32.7 Public-Private Collaboration in AI Governance

Collaboration between the public and private sectors is essential for effective AI governance. The chapter concludes by emphasizing the importance of public-private partnerships in developing and implementing AI governance policies. By fostering collaboration, policymakers can leverage diverse expertise, resources, and perspectives to create a governance framework that promotes responsible AI development and benefits society as a whole.

CHAPTER 33: AI AND HUMAN RIGHTS: NAVIGATING ETHICAL BOUNDARIES

33.1 The Intersection of AI and Human Rights

AI technologies have a profound impact on human rights, introducing both opportunities and challenges. This chapter explores the intersection of AI and human rights, addressing ethical considerations related to privacy, freedom of expression, non-discrimination, and the broader implications for individuals and communities.

33.2 Privacy Rights in the Age of AI

The extensive use of AI in data processing raises significant concerns about privacy rights. This section examines the ethical considerations related to privacy in the age of AI, discussing the potential impact of AI technologies on individual privacy and strategies for safeguarding privacy rights in the face of technological advancements.

33.3 Freedom of Expression and AI

AI's influence on content moderation and information dissemination poses challenges to freedom of expression. This part of the chapter explores the ethical considerations related to freedom of expression in the context of AI, discussing issues such as censorship, algorithmic biases, and the responsible use of AI to preserve and protect this fundamental human right.

33.4 Non-Discrimination and Bias in AI Systems

The potential for bias in AI systems raises concerns about discrimination and inequality. This section examines the ethical considerations related to non-discrimination in AI, discussing strategies for identifying and mitigating biases to ensure that AI technologies do not perpetuate or exacerbate societal inequalities.

33.5 Protecting Human Rights in AI-assisted Decision-making

AI-assisted decision-making processes can impact various human rights, including the right to a fair trial and due process. This chapter explores the ethical considerations related to protecting human rights in AI-assisted decision-making, discussing issues such as transparency, accountability, and the responsible use of AI in legal and judicial contexts.

33.6 Ensuring Inclusivity and Accessibility

AI technologies must be designed to ensure inclusivity and accessibility for all individuals, regardless of background or abilities. This section examines the ethical considerations related to inclusivity and accessibility in the development and deployment of AI, discussing strategies for promoting diverse perspectives and addressing potential barriers to access.

33.7 Human Rights Impact Assessments for AI Technologies

The chapter concludes by exploring the concept of human rights impact assessments for AI technologies. It discusses the importance of assessing the potential impact of AI on human rights, providing a framework for organizations and policymakers to proactively identify, address, and mitigate any adverse effects on individuals and communities.

CHAPTER 34: AI AND ENVIRONMENTAL SUSTAINABILITY: ETHICAL CONSIDERATIONS

34.1 The Environmental Impact of AI Technologies

As AI technologies become more pervasive, their environmental impact raises ethical considerations. This chapter explores the intersection of AI and environmental sustainability, addressing the potential environmental challenges associated with the development, deployment, and use of AI, and proposing strategies for mitigating these impacts.

34.2 Energy Consumption and Carbon Footprint

The energy consumption of AI systems, particularly large-scale models and data centers, contributes to their carbon footprint. This section examines the ethical considerations related to energy consumption and carbon emissions in AI technologies, discussing strategies for optimizing energy efficiency and adopting sustainable practices in AI development.

34.3 E-Waste and Responsible AI Hardware

The rapid pace of technological advancements in AI hardware

contributes to electronic waste (e-waste) concerns. This part of the chapter explores the ethical considerations related to e-waste generated by AI hardware, discussing the importance of responsible design, recycling initiatives, and the development of sustainable hardware solutions in the AI industry.

34.4 Resource Extraction and Ethical Sourcing

The materials used in the production of AI hardware may involve resource extraction with ethical implications. This section examines the ethical considerations related to resource extraction and sourcing of materials for AI technologies, discussing strategies for ethical procurement, responsible supply chain practices, and reducing the environmental impact of resource extraction.

34.5 AI for Environmental Monitoring and Conservation

While AI can contribute to environmental monitoring and conservation efforts, its deployment must be guided by ethical principles. This chapter explores the ethical considerations in using AI for environmental purposes, discussing issues such as data privacy, community engagement, and the responsible use of AI to support sustainable practices in environmental monitoring and conservation.

34.6 Circular Economy Principles in AI Development

The concept of a circular economy, where resources are used more efficiently and waste is minimized, can be applied to AI development. This section examines how circular economy principles can be integrated into AI development, emphasizing the importance of product longevity, reuse of components, and sustainable practices to reduce the environmental impact of AI technologies.

34.7 Collaboration for Sustainable AI Practices

The chapter concludes by highlighting the importance

of collaboration among AI developers, policymakers, and environmental experts to promote sustainable AI practices. By working together, stakeholders can develop ethical guidelines, share best practices, and implement strategies that prioritize both technological advancement and environmental sustainability in the AI industry.

CHAPTER 35: AI AND HEALTHCARE: NAVIGATING ETHICAL FRONTIERS

35.1 The Transformative Impact of AI on Healthcare

AI technologies hold immense potential to revolutionize healthcare, but their integration raises ethical considerations that require careful navigation. This chapter explores the intersection of AI and healthcare, addressing ethical challenges and opportunities in areas such as diagnostics, treatment, patient privacy, and the overall impact on the healthcare ecosystem.

35.2 Ethical Considerations in AI-assisted Diagnostics

The use of AI in diagnostic processes, including medical imaging and pathology, introduces ethical considerations related to accuracy, transparency, and patient trust. This section examines the ethical dimensions of AI-assisted diagnostics, discussing issues such as accountability, human-AI collaboration, and ensuring that diagnostic tools prioritize patient well-being.

35.3 Treatment and Personalized Medicine with AI

AI has the potential to enhance personalized medicine by tailoring treatments to individual patient characteristics. This part of the chapter explores the ethical considerations in AI-driven treatment decisions, including issues related to informed consent, data privacy, and the responsible integration of AI in treatment planning for better patient outcomes.

35.4 Patient Privacy and Data Security in AI Healthcare

The collection and analysis of patient data by AI systems raise ethical concerns about privacy and data security. This section examines the ethical considerations related to patient privacy in AI healthcare, discussing strategies for safeguarding sensitive health information, obtaining informed consent, and ensuring transparent data practices.

35.5 Bias and Fairness in Healthcare AI

AI algorithms used in healthcare may exhibit biases, impacting the fairness and equity of healthcare outcomes. This chapter explores the ethical considerations related to bias and fairness in healthcare AI, discussing strategies for identifying and mitigating biases to ensure that AI technologies contribute to equitable healthcare for diverse patient populations.

35.6 Ethical Challenges in AI-driven Clinical Decision Support

The use of AI in clinical decision support systems introduces ethical challenges related to the role of AI in medical decision-making. This section examines the ethical considerations in AI-driven clinical decision support, addressing issues such as accountability, transparency, and the responsible deployment of AI technologies to support healthcare professionals in their decision-making processes.

35.7 Ensuring Equity in AI Healthcare Applications

The chapter concludes by emphasizing the importance of ensuring equity in AI healthcare applications. It discusses the ethical imperative of addressing healthcare disparities, promoting inclusivity, and leveraging AI technologies to advance healthcare outcomes for all individuals, regardless of socio-economic background or demographic factors.

CHAPTER 36: AI IN EDUCATION: BALANCING INNOVATION AND ETHICAL CONSIDERATIONS

36.1 The Role of AI in Transforming Education

The integration of AI in education has the potential to revolutionize learning experiences, but it also raises ethical considerations that must be carefully navigated. This chapter explores the intersection of AI and education, addressing ethical challenges and opportunities in areas such as personalized learning, assessment, student privacy, and the overall impact on educational systems.

36.2 Personalized Learning and Ethical Considerations

AI-driven personalized learning systems offer tailored educational experiences, but they come with ethical considerations related to data privacy, algorithmic biases, and the potential impact on student well-being. This section examines the ethical dimensions of personalized learning, discussing issues such as transparency, informed consent, and responsible AI use to enhance educational outcomes.

36.3 Assessments and Fairness in AI Education

AI technologies play a role in educational assessments, introducing ethical challenges related to fairness, accountability, and the potential for biases in evaluation. This part of the chapter explores the ethical considerations in AI-driven educational assessments, discussing strategies for ensuring fairness, mitigating biases, and promoting equitable educational opportunities for all students.

36.4 Student Privacy and Data Security in AI Education

The use of AI in education involves the collection and analysis of student data, raising ethical concerns about privacy and data security. This section examines the ethical considerations related to student privacy in AI education, discussing the importance of transparent data practices, informed consent, and safeguards to protect sensitive student information.

36.5 Addressing Socio-economic Disparities in AI Education

AI in education has the potential to either exacerbate or mitigate socio-economic disparities in learning opportunities. This chapter explores the ethical considerations related to addressing socio-economic inequalities in AI education, discussing strategies for promoting inclusivity, accessibility, and leveraging AI to bridge educational gaps among diverse student populations.

36.6 Ethical Use of AI in Educational Decision-making

AI technologies may play a role in educational decision-making processes, from student placement to resource allocation. This section examines the ethical considerations in AI-driven educational decision-making, addressing issues such as transparency, accountability, and the responsible use of AI to support fair and just educational policies.

36.7 Nurturing Ethical Digital Citizenship through AI Education

The chapter concludes by emphasizing the importance of nurturing ethical digital citizenship through AI education. It discusses the ethical imperative of educating students about AI technologies, promoting critical thinking, and fostering responsible digital behaviors to prepare the next generation for ethical engagement with AI in various aspects of their lives.